Broken Metronome

POEMS BY

Connie Post

GLASS LYRE PRESS

Design & Layout: Steven Asmussen
Cover Art: Paula Golightly
Author Photo :   Casey Henshaw Little Rae Photography

Glass Lyre Press, LLC
P.O. Box 2693
Glenview, IL 60025
www.GlassLyrePress.com

Broken

Metronome

"Do not go gentle into that good night"
Dylan Thomas

For my brother Cliff. Always with us.

CONTENTS

◇

Underwater

At swim lessons
in the community pool
we clung to the same ledge
kicking our feet
listening intently to our instructor
while elbowing each other
under the water

I watched the teacher
I watched her so intently
that when I looked over to my right
you were suddenly
submerged

I didn't understand
until then
what it meant
to come close to drowning

I saw your face
and maybe you saw mine

you sank lower and lower
until a swift hand plunged in
and pulled you out
of those chlorinated depths

you came out sputtering

we never spoke of it
after that

I didn't think of it much
until today

until I sign into
the front desk of the nursing facility

I poke my head into your room
watch the way the Parkinson's
pulls you under

I sit by your bedside
this time my whole self
plunges in

this time
we both hang on

Searching

Scientists
search for a cause

all I can do
is comb the
literature
like a student
cramming for exams

trying to map the way back
to your first symptom

how can we know
what decisions
a body will make
for us

how can we know
how long a mutation
will keep a secret

how can we know
where your mind is
when you no longer
speak

all I can hold onto
is the memory
of your hand in mine
when we first went to
Sunday school

and believed
in everything

End Stage

Maybe someday soon
I won't say "hospice"
every day

or won't ask how much
you have eaten today

or if there has been another
hallucination
or if food is again
stuck in your throat

"your brother
is in end stage Parkinson's"
the doctors say

but they won't say
"your younger brother"
but I say it to myself
every time I close
your bedroom door

every night
I count my breaths
before I go to sleep
as if I can count yours too

Saturday, you ate little bites
of the gingerbread cookies
I made

Sunday, I read you *Wild Geese*
by Mary Oliver
then I sing *Moon River*
you don't know that today
is winter solstice

the Christmas lights
in our town
flicker off and on
like your eyes

Parkinson's Glossary

Ataxia
a movement disorder
marked by loss of balance

    you fell again today

Dementia
a decline in memory
of intellectual functioning

    friends ask
    "isn't he too young for that"

Facial Masking
the face is immobile with reduced blinking

    I wonder what you are thinking
    I hope you can hear me

Hypokinesia
slow or diminished movement

    I try to move slowly with you
    like when we practiced for the
    seventh-grade dance

Rigidity
abnormal stiffness in a limb
or other body part

    I tell you to remember
    how you felt when
    you rode your bike
    every weekend

Dopamine Antagonist
a class of drugs commonly prescribed
in Parkinson's disease that bind
to dopamine receptors and
mimic dopamine's actions in the brain

>   you've been given everything
>   that can be given
>   the doctors say

End of Life Care
care given to people who are near the end of life
and have stopped treatment
to cure or control their disease

>   you,
>   a bed,
>   and music
>   you used to love

Coming in the Front Door

Your caretaker tells me
a woman in your group home
died yesterday

I didn't know her
but I pass by the room
and her empty bed

her keening
permeated every corner
of the house

I enter your room
knowing you are losing your appetite
"Parkinson's is a thief"
I say to myself

the new hospice nurse asks me
"remind me, how old is your brother?"

we struggle with medication schedules
and what to change

less suffering
less suffering

that's all we seem to say these days

but only the dimming light
seems to know the answer

I help you sort through
a thousand hallucinations
as I walk inside
those long corridors
with you

the truth hides
in the small cracks of twilight

Orthostatic Hypotension

When you sit or stand up
your blood pressure
plummets

but every day you fight
to get up
you don't care
what the nurses say

"I have to get out of here"
you repeat over and over
and then pull off the bed sheets
and start to rise

I try all my
"stay in bed" tricks
I used when my children were young

but there is no story
or fairytale I can read to you
that will ease this cerebral storm

you continue the fight
until I say
"you will get out of here eventually"
and then immediately
I feel guilty for the lie

how many ways
can someone fall off
the ledge of themselves

now that you are finally asleep
I stand in the doorway
watching for signs
of impending rockslides

keeping an eye out
for the first loose pebble

Two Miles Apart

I drive between the two places
ignoring the gas gauge
and the narrowing roads

my son in one group home
my brother in another

my son has never spoken,
autism took his language
decades ago

my brother's voice fades away
like a church bell in the distance

I stop at a park along the way
the grass tamped down
from a kid's bike
small signs of loss
and its insidious tracks

I will bring my brother
good food and music he likes
but he will turn away
once the hospice nurse arrives

I will bring my son
a coke with extra ice
and he will drink it all
in a few minutes

each time I visit
I hurry through each yellow light
knowing there isn't enough time

but I make my way between
these two quiet countries
finding tranquil roads
with low hanging trees and
small silent creatures
who show me the way

Bedside

I don't count your respirations
per minute any longer

I don't look at the little blue
hospice book
that spells out the shades
of your illness

an ending
is an ending
no matter how the minutes
drip by

It's the middle of the week
I put on my N95 mask
and sit close to you

I turn on the same soft piano music
and the notes float
next to the absence
of our conversation

I read that dementia patients
hold onto old memories

so I enter the realm
of fifty years ago
and take you with me

I talk about the tadpoles
we used to find
the dinosaur trails we made
in the backyard dirt
and about GI Joe
when dying was only pretend

Hallucinations

I bought you a new
blanket this week

I thought you'd like the rectangle
patterns in a soft brown

but a few days later
you are terrified of everything
even the blanket
is calling your name

I sit by your bed
and make sure you know
those footsteps down the hall
are not coming for you

that the curtains
are not a shadow self

I hold your hand and tell you
"I am here and won't let
anything hurt you"

soon
we can only put
white sheets on the bed

the terror of patterns
barges through the front door
of your dementia

I want to cradle your brain
in my hands

I want to stand at the gateway
of your disease
and make sure its glare
never makes eye contact

two weeks later
we take down all the photos on the wall
you used to love

Contracture

"A fixed tightening of muscle,
tendons, ligaments, or skin.
It prevents normal movement
of the associated body part"

the nurse increased the dose
of your fentanyl patch today

it will take up to 48 hours
to take effect

in the meantime
you continue with
breakthrough doses
of morphine

I think about the small
gathering of trees
outside your window

I wonder if at dusk
they secretly tell you
how to keep your limbs
intact
and yet
learn to bend
with the wind

Ode to Language

You've stopped speaking

I know all too well
that silence makes its own rules

I understand
how a word
is a story caught in the throat

I see how a sentence
is the long shadow
halfway across
a small room

I nod
in silent understanding
when your mouth moves
but nothing comes out

how often
do we pretend to know
what another says to us
when they are
falling from a cliff

instead
I crouch down
hold an arm over
a rocky ledge

and hope you grab hold

Italian Food

All through your illness
I make you lasagna

sometimes I stay up late
making sure the sauce is perfect

sometimes I boil the noodles
a little longer than I should

I don't measure the thyme
or sage or garlic
I let our heritage
show me the way

I use four kinds of cheese
and think of you in each layer

your caretaker tells me
"he will only eat your food now"

I bring you pasta on weekends
and Wednesdays
whenever you are close to running out

I believed for a while
I could keep you alive that way

but we all know
your doctor gave you at most
six months

the day you stop eating
I am at the grocery store
buying ingredients

I leave abruptly
and watch the day devour itself

your disease is a glutton
who can't consume
enough of you

Respiration Explained

The hospice nurse gives
it a name
Cheyne-Stokes breathing

an abnormal breathing pattern
where the patient
has fast shallow breaths
then deep heavy ones

she explains it's the body's way
of "trying to correct itself"
when everything is shutting down.

for days we watch you
fall in and out of the cadence
of endings.

the nurse says it's not painful
but it's hard for me to believe
as I watch you fall in and out
of the broken metronome
of a fatal disease

I say your name quietly
several times an hour
and although you don't respond
I remind myself that
the literature says
"they can hear you
even when they are unconscious"

I remind you of all the times
we collected
daddy long leg spiders
how at times
you held them in your hand

each one pushing up
against an unknown surface
as we all do

This page
intentionally left blank

to mark
the moment of your passing

It's Been One Week

Since you died

and so it begins
the counting
months, days
and years
without a brother

as if the counting
can contain the loss

as if somehow
it helps me
measure the
immeasurable

I walk in my neighborhood
and although you
never walked these streets with me
they seem somehow emptier
or my footsteps are heavier
I am not sure which

I only know
that one year
minus a week is
fifty-one weeks

maybe soon
I will only rely on integers
numbers not divisible of themselves
to understand how to let you go

until then
the dusk waits for me

after the dog is finally asleep
I flick on the bedroom lamp
and find the secret abacus under my bed
slowly teaching me
how to count myself backwards
to you

The Last Time We Played Chess

I threw a rook at you
before I stomped out of the room
we were teenagers

now that you are gone
I can't stop thinking about
your quiet approach
placing each pawn out
one by one

I watched your fingers lightly
touch the chess pieces
showing how you understood
the intricate balance
in the power of the board

I think of your fingers
in the last year of your life
clinging onto the bed rails

how I placed your hands gently
on your blanket after you'd gone to sleep

how could we have known then
that death had its own strategy

how could I have known
how regret jumps over everything else
like the knights on the board

I no longer play the game
I am no longer willing to glue together
broken bishops and bereft kings

I fold the chessboard
the way I sometimes close a book
before it's over
dog-earing the pages
as if I will remember
the way back

Obligations to a Towel

Make sure you rinse yourself twice
so the sorrow from your pores
does not catch on the tiny threads

pretend the surface is soft enough
to slide past the regret
of your hips and knees

make sure
you understand absorption –
how a towel
must live a life
wrapped around you

look inside the layers
of the green terry cloth
remember how you loved it once
how the cashier said
"great color"
before she placed it into the bag

look at the towel again
after dusk
and find the way it tells you
the shower water is contaminated

negotiate with dampness
pretend there is enough
time to dry everything

How to Dust the Sorrow from Your Room

Start with the ceiling
it's hiding there
and will fall to the ground
if you nudge it

it's not under the bed
or the old lamp

it's in the place
you never look
where your old shoes
are stacked

it's in the tracks of the sliding door
it's at the edge of the dresser

it's where your memories
sift through you
when you fall asleep

wait until the house
is as dark as the closet
of your body

Slowly sweep
with the bristles
of your hands

find everything you detest
and make it holy again

Two Days

After the funeral
I go to your gravesite
there are hundreds
of white flowers from the service
scattered atop the small rise in the grass
where your coffin is

I say a few words
but the nearby family
feels too close

so I pretend instead
I am by your bedside again
whispering words to you
that I hoped would
seep into your quiet coma

in our last seven days
I came to your room,
pulled up the same chair
and put my hand through
the bars on the bed and told you
"it's okay to go when you're ready"

you died on a Sunday morning
since then
I have kept our secret stories
in my left pocket
along with all the things
I could not say

I think about how sometimes
peace and death go together
how one assembles the other

dusk is coming
I head for my car
the flowers on your grave
are starting to wilt

the petals
pulling themselves
slowly away
from the stems

Late May Visit

I went to your gravesite today

the tombstone isn't there yet

I dread that day
when permanence
finds me
like a gray stone

I dread it
like the day
I waited three hours for the coroner
to come and take you away

that day sticks to me
heavy like a lead apron
I think now
of how I stopped the coroner
just before he left
and said "can you wait just a minute"

I put my hand on your silent body
and said "safe travels, brother"
and now I wonder
what light years really mean

my astronomer friend
tells me that the stars we see now
appear as they did
four thousand years ago

how can we travel so far
but end up at the same
clearing in the grass

At Last

Summer has found me
I'm supposed to be
healing

I am supposed to be
doing self-care

I am supposed to
go back
to the routines
I had before
hospice

instead
I am driving up the hill
where you used to ride your bike
finding all the small
vista points
where you must have stopped
for a long drink of water

Robin Red Breast

All through your illness
I wake to the sound of birds

I ignore them

I don't care about the
type, kind, species
or if they are far or near

I just get dressed
and drive to see you

two months after you die
a red breasted robin
makes a nest in the hanging plant
just outside my bedroom window

I watch her carefully
I go to the window
countless times a day
and make sure everything is okay

I worry at night
about the eggs
and if they will still
be there in the morning

I read grief books
I watch mindfulness videos

nothing helps

It's a Sunday in June
I watch her until noon
she stares ahead
doing her silent work

I see now
how someone comes back to you
often times
in a small shelter
just beyond your reach

Acknowledgements

Third Wednesday Magazine: "Shallow Breath"

About the Author

Connie Post served as the first Poet Laureate of Livermore from 2005 to 2009. During that time, she wrote over twenty five poems of occasion for civic events. She also created two popular reading series. Post's poems appear widely in magazines such as *The American Journal of Poetry, 2 River, Calyx, Dogwood, Blue Fifth Review, Two Bridges Review, Comstock Review, Spoon River Poetry Review, River Styx, Crab Creek Review, Slipstream, The Big Muddy, Slippery Elm, Valparaiso Poetry Review* and *Verse Daily*. Her first full length collection, *Floodwater* was published in 2014 by Glass Lyre Press and won the Lyrebird Award. Her chapbook *And When the Sun Drops* won the 2012 Aurorean Editor's chapbook prize. Her second full length collection, *Prime Meridian* was published by Glass Lyre Press in 2020, and was named a distinguished favorite in the Independent Press Awards. It was also a finalist in the Best Book Awards and the International Book Awards. Her most recent full length collection, *Between Twilight* was published by New York Quarterly Books in 2023.

Her work has appeared in several anthologies, including *Alongside we Travel - Contemporary Poets on Autism* (NYQ Books, 2019), *Collateral Damage* and *Carrying the Branch* (Glass Lyre Press) and *Truth to Power Writers Respond To The Rhetoric Of Hate And Fear* (Cutthroat Magazine), *The Aeolian Harp Anthology Series* (2021), *Though the Ash, New Leaves* (Cutthroat Magazine 2022)

Her poetry awards include the 2018 Liakoura Award, the Crab Creek Review Poetry Award, the Caesura Award and the Prick of the Spindle Poetry Competition. In addition, she won second place for the Jack Kerouac Poetry Prize and the Atticus Review Poetry Prize.

Glass Lyre Press

exceptional works to replenish the spirit

Glass Lyre Press is an independent literary publisher interested in technically accomplished, stylistically distinct, and original work. Glass Lyre seeks diverse writers that possess a dynamic aesthetic and an ability to emotionally and intellectually engage a wide audience of readers.

Glass Lyre's vision is to connect the world through language and art. We hope to expand the scope of poetry and short fiction for the general reader through exceptionally well-written books, which evoke emotion, provide insight, and resonate with the human spirit.

Poetry Collections
Poetry Chapbooks
Select Short & Flash Fiction
Anthologies

www.GlassLyrePress.com

9 781941 783962